May all your future years be free
From disappointment, care or strife,
That every birthday you will be
A little more in love with life.

Happy Birthday

To

Claire Jackson

From

Cynthia Robertson

Happy Birthday

BY

BARBARA MILO OHRBACH

Cheerful Wishes, Warm Thoughts,
and Delightful Recipes
that Celebrate Your Special Day

CLARKSON POTTER/PUBLISHERS
NEW YORK

Design by Justine Strasberg   Endpapers by Harry Singer

Every effort has been made to locate the copyright holders of materials used in this book. Should there by omissions or errors, we apologize and shall be pleased to make the appropriate acknowledgments in future editions.

Grateful acknowledgment is given for permission to reprint "First Fig" by Edna St. Vincent Millay. From *Collected Poems*, HarperCollins. Copyright © 1922, 1950 by Edna St. Vincent Millay. Reprinted by permission of Elizabeth Barnett, literary executor.

Published by Clarkson N. Potter, Inc., 201 East 50th Street, New York, New York 10022. Member of the Crown Publishing Group.

Random House, Inc. New York, Toronto, London, Sydney, Auckland

CLARKSON N. POTTER, POTTER, and colophon are trademarks of Clarkson N. Potter, Inc.

Manufactured in Hong Kong

Calligraphy by Tim Girvin

Library of Congress Cataloging-in-Publication Data
Happy birthday / [compiled] by Barbara Milo Ohrbach.—1st ed.
1. Birthdays—Quotations, maxims, etc.   I. Ohrbach, Barbara Milo.
PN6084.B5H16   1994
808.88'2—dc20   93-25256
CIP
ISBN 0-517-58625-8

10 9 8 7 6 5 4 3 2 1

First Edition

Table of Contents

A grateful thank you to everyone here for their help in putting this book together: Beth Allen, Gayle Benderoff, Deborah Geltman, Tim Girvin, Teresa Nicholas, Mel Ohrbach, Ed Otto, Andrea Peabbles, Harry Singer, Tina Strasberg, Lisa Tow, Jane Treuhaft, and Shirley Wohl.

Introduction

JANUARY
GARNET
CONSTANCY

FEBRUARY
AMETHYST
SINCERITY

MARCH
TRUE   FIRM
BLOODSTONE

Everybody has one.'' Writer Russell Baker included this line in one of his recent columns about birthdays. And as you will see from the quotes in this little book, everybody approaches his or her big day differently.

As we get older, the delight with which we always welcomed birthdays is sometimes replaced by other feelings—some not quite so welcome! Perhaps we all need to remind

APRIL
DIAMOND INNOCENCE

MAY
EMERALD
HAPPINESS

JUNE
PEARL
HEALTH

JULY
RUBY LOVE

AUGUST
SARDONYX
FELICITY

SEPTEMBER
SAPPHIRE
WISDOM

ourselves that birthdays can be a celebration of
many things, as expressed by the following
words:

*"Have you ever thought that the candles on a
birthday cake can represent accomplishments as
well as years? The little things we've done to
help others—perhaps a thoughtful prayer, an
encouraging word or a helping hand when it was
needed. . . . Each candle on our birthday cake,
therefore, can be a symbol of what we have done to
enrich the lives of others as well as our own."*

As you browse through this book, I hope
that this thought and the others included in its
pages will make you smile a little, inspire you to
think a bit, and help you to cheerfully look
forward to all your birthdays to come. And
keep in mind these words of Ralph Waldo
Emerson:

*"Write on your hearts that everyday is the best
day of the year."*

Barbara Milo Ohrbach

OCTOBER
OPAL HOPE

NOVEMBER
TOPAZ
FIDELITY

DECEMBER
TURQUOISE
SUCCESS

The secret of staying young is to live honestly, eat slowly, and lie about your age.

LUCILLE BALL

Age is strictly a case of mind over matter. If you don't mind, it doesn't matter.

JACK BENNY

The old believe everything; the middle-aged suspect everything; the young know everything.

OSCAR WILDE

There are so many things about which some old man ought to tell one while one is little; for when one is grown one would know them as a matter of course.

RAINER MARIA RILKE

Pleas'd to look forward, pleas'd to look behind,
And count each birthday with a grateful mind.

ALEXANDER POPE

Whatever with the past has gone,
The best is always yet to come.

LUCY LARCOM

It takes a long time
to grow young.

PABLO PICASSO

It is better to wear out than to rust out.

BISHOP RICHARD CUMBERLAND

7

January

BIRTHSTONE — *Garnet: Constancy*
FLOWER — *Carnation*
COLORS — *Black and Dark Blue*
CAPRICORN — *December 22 to January 21*
AQUARIUS — *January 22 to February 19*

January's the month to start aright
So the rest of the year may be happy and bright.

Sunshine Cake

1 CUP SIFTED CAKE
  FLOUR
½ TEASPOON SALT
6 LARGE EGGS AND
  3 EXTRA EGG WHITES
1⅔ CUPS SUGAR

2 TABLESPOONS FRESH
  ORANGE JUICE
1 TABLESPOON GRATED
  LEMON PEEL
1 TEASPOON CREAM OF
  TARTAR

❧ Preheat oven to 350° F. Set out a 10-inch angel food cake pan.

❧ Sift the flour with the salt.

❧ Separate the 6 eggs. Using an electric mixer, beat the yolks for 5 minutes or until thick.

❧ Gradually add 1 cup of sugar, beating 5 minutes more. Add juice and lemon peel.

❧ In another bowl, beat the 9 egg whites with the cream of tartar until frothy. Beat in the remaining ⅔ cup sugar until stiff but not dry.

❧ Fold ⅓ of the whites into the yolk mixture. Fold in the flour, then the remaining egg whites. Spoon into the pan.

❧ Bake 35 minutes or until tester comes out clean.

❧ Let cool in the pan, inverting the cake, top down, until cold. Then remove.

MAKES 12 SERVINGS

A diplomat is a man who always remembers a woman's birthday but never remembers her age.

ROBERT FROST

Greetings

"My birth-day"—what a different sound
That word had in my youthful ears!

THOMAS MOORE

Here's a posy of flowers, and a basket too,
With Birthday greetings all for you.

ANONYMOUS

EVERY
GOOD WISH

Would ye both eat your cake and have your cake?

JOHN HEYWOOD

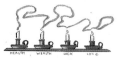

There are two ways of spreading light: to be the candle or the mirror that reflects it.

EDITH WHARTON

Most of us can remember a time when a birthday—especially if it was one's own—brightened the world as if a second sun had risen.

ROBERT LYND

I remember, I remember
The roses, red and white,
The violets, and the lily-cups,
Those flowers made of light!
The lilacs, where the robin built,
And where my brother set
The laburnum on his birthday,—
The tree is living yet.

THOMAS HOOD

The best way to remember your wife's birthday is to forget it once.

H. V. PROCHNOW

Greetings

It is lovely, when I forget all birthdays, including my own, to find that somebody remembers me.

ELLEN GLASGOW

February

BIRTHSTONE — *Amethyst: Sincerity*
FLOWER — *Violet*
COLORS — *Light Blue and Yellow*
AQUARIUS — *January 22 to February 19*
PISCES — *February 20 to March 20*

12

February brings thoughts of hearts and flowers;
May it bring you many happy hours.

Ice-cream Roll

1 RECIPE SUNSHINE CAKE
  BATTER (page 9)
¼ CUP SIFTED
  CONFECTIONERS'
  SUGAR

1 QUART ICE CREAM,
  SOFTENED

🍃 Preheat oven to 350° F. Butter a standard jelly-roll pan and line the bottom with waxed paper. Have a clean towel ready.

🍃 Prepare Sunshine Cake batter and spread evenly in the pan. Bake 15 minutes or until the top springs back.

🍃 Spread out the towel and sprinkle with confectioners' sugar. Immediately invert the cake onto the towel. Carefully remove the waxed paper. Using a serrated knife, trim away the four hard edges of the cake.

🍃 Starting from the narrow end, quickly roll up the cake in the towel and place on a rack to cool completely (several hours at least).

🍃 Gently unroll the cake and spread it with the softened ice cream, leaving a 1-inch margin on all sides. Discard towel. Roll up cake, wrap it in the waxed paper, and freeze until firm.

🍃 To serve, slice crosswise with a serrated knife into 1-inch-thick pieces.

MAKES 8 SERVINGS

At times it seems that I am living my life backward, and that at the approach of old age my real youth will begin. My soul was born covered with wrinkles—wrinkles that my ancestors and parents most assiduously put there and that I had the greatest trouble removing, . . .

ANDRÉ GIDE

Youth is happy because it has the ability to see beauty. Anyone who keeps the ability to see beauty never grows old.

FRANZ KAFKA

You'd scarce expect one of my age
To speak in public on the stage,
And if I chance to fall below
Demosthenes or Cicero,
Don't view me with a critic's eye,
But pass my imperfections by.
Large streams from little fountains flow,
Tall oaks from little acorns grow.

DAVID EVERETT

One of the signs of passing youth is the birth of a sense of fellowship with other human beings as we take our place among them.

VIRGINIA WOOLF

Youth comes but once in a lifetime.

HENRY WADSWORTH LONGFELLOW

Youth had been a habit of hers for so long that she could not part with it.

RUDYARD KIPLING

Keep true to the dreams of thy youth.

FRIEDRICH VON SCHILLER

It is through the idealism of youth that man catches sight of truth, and in that idealism he possesses a wealth which he must never exchange for anything else.

ALBERT SCHWEITZER

March

BIRTHSTONE — *Bloodstone: Courage*
FLOWER — *Jonquil*
COLOR — *White*
PISCES — *February 20 to March 20*
ARIES — *March 21 to April 20*

March with its winds so fierce is here;
May it blow good luck is my wish sincere.

Quick Party Pizza

2 TABLESPOONS CORNMEAL

1 ROLL (10 OUNCES) PREPARED PIZZA DOUGH

1 JAR (14 OUNCES) CHUNKY TOMATO SAUCE

2 TEASPOONS DRIED ITALIAN HERBS

CHOICE OF TOPPINGS:
SAUTÉED BELL PEPPERS, MUSHROOMS OR ONIONS
SLICED PEPPERONI OR SAUSAGE

2 CUPS SHREDDED MOZZARELLA CHEESE

2 TABLESPOONS OLIVE OIL

❧ Preheat oven to 425° F. Oil an 18 × 15-inch baking sheet. Dust with cornmeal.

❧ Unroll the dough onto the baking sheet and press it out, working from the center to the edges. Pinch the edges to stand up slightly.

❧ Mix the tomato sauce with the Italian herbs and spread over the dough.

❧ Top with your choice of toppings, then sprinkle with the cheese and olive oil.

❧ Bake for 15 minutes or until crust is golden.

MAKES 1 PIZZA THAT SERVES 8

A man over ninety is a great comfort to all his elderly neighbors: he is a picket-guard at the extreme outpost; and the young folks of sixty and seventy feel that the enemy must get by him before he can come near their camp.

OLIVER WENDELL HOLMES

90

Everything I know I learned after I was thirty.

GEORGES CLEMENCEAU

30

The years between fifty and seventy are the hardest. You are always being asked to do things, and yet you are not decrepit enough to turn them down.

T. S. ELIOT

18

From birth to age eighteen, a girl needs good parents. From eighteen to thirty-five, she needs good looks. From thirty-five to fifty-five, she needs a good personality. From fifty-five on, she needs good cash.

SOPHIE TUCKER

W*hen you turn thirty, a whole new thing happens: you see yourself acting like your parents.*

BLAIR SABOL

W*hen I was a boy of fourteen, my father was so ignorant I could hardly stand to have the old man around. But when I got to be twenty-one, I was astonished at how much he had learned in seven years.*

MARK TWAIN

T*he advantage of being eighty years old is that one has had many people to love.*

JEAN RENOIR

N*ature gives you the face you have at twenty, but it's up to you to merit the face you have at fifty.*

COCO CHANEL

April

BIRTHSTONE — *Diamond: Innocence*
FLOWER — *Sweet Pea*
COLORS — *Yellow and Red*
ARIES — *March 21 to April 20*
TAURUS — *April 21 to May 21*

20

April's the month of sunshine and showers;
Happy thoughts sent with springtime flowers.

Double Fudge Cake

6 SQUARES
  UNSWEETENED BAKING
  CHOCOLATE
3 CUPS SIFTED CAKE
  FLOUR
1 TABLESPOON
  BAKING POWDER
½ TEASPOON SALT

½ TEASPOON BAKING
  SODA
1 CUP BUTTER
2 CUPS SUGAR
6 LARGE EGGS
1 TEASPOON VANILLA
1¼ CUPS MILK
1 CUP SOUR CREAM

🐦 Preheat oven to 350° F. Butter three 9-inch round pans and line bottoms with waxed paper.

🐦 Melt the chocolate over low heat and cool.

🐦 Sift the flour with the baking powder, salt, and baking soda.

🐦 Using an electric mixer, cream the butter and sugar. Separate the eggs. Beat in the yolks, one at a time, then the chocolate and vanilla.

🐦 Stir in the flour mixture, alternating with the milk. Fold in the sour cream.

🐦 In another bowl, beat the egg whites until stiff. Gently fold into the chocolate mixture. Spoon evenly into pans.

🐦 Bake 35 minutes or until tester comes out clean. Cool on rack for 5 minutes. Remove from pans and cool completely.

🐦 Frost each layer and sides with Fluffy Fudge Frosting on page 25.

MAKES 12 SERVINGS

How far that little candle throws his beams!
WILLIAM SHAKESPEARE

If you want to be happy, be.
HENRY DAVID THOREAU

The secret anniversaries of the heart.
HENRY WADSWORTH LONGFELLOW

Never look a gift horse in the mouth!
SAINT JEROME

God loveth a cheerful giver.
CORINTHIANS

The manner of giving is worth more than the gift.
PIERRE CORNEILLE

M_y heart is like a singing bird. . . .
Because the birthday of my life
Is come, my love is come to me.

CHRISTINA ROSSETTI

"I mean, what is an un-birthday present?"
"A present given when it isn't your birthday,
of course."

Alice considered a little. "I like birthday
presents best," she said at last.

"You don't know what you're talking
about!" cried Humpty Dumpty. "How many
days are there in a year?"

"Three hundred and sixty-five," said Alice.
"And how many birthdays have you?"
"One."

LEWIS CARROLL

I want to be an artist
To paint pictures just for you,
So when each birthday comes around,
I can send you quite a few.

ANONYMOUS

May

BIRTHSTONE — *Emerald: Success in Love*
FLOWER — *Lily of the Valley*
COLORS — *Yellow and Red*
TAURUS — *April 21 to May 21*
GEMINI — *May 22 to June 21*

May brings the lambkins that frolic and play;
Here's a wish that you be happy and gay.

Fluffy Fudge Frosting

1½ CUPS BUTTER
6 SQUARES UNSWEETENED BAKING CHOCOLATE
3 LARGE EGG WHITES

2 CUPS SIFTED CONFECTIONERS' SUGAR
1 TEASPOON VANILLA

✦ Soften the butter to room temperature.

✖ Melt the chocolate over low heat and cool.

✦ Using an electric mixer, beat the egg whites in a small bowl until stiff.

✦ Continue to beat, gradually adding the sugar until the frosting is thick.

✖ In another bowl, using the electric mixer, cream the butter with the vanilla, beating constantly. Add the egg-white mixture, then the chocolate, beating constantly for 3 minutes or until fluffy.

✖ Use to frost Double Fudge Cake on page 21.

MAKES ENOUGH FROSTING FOR
ONE 3-LAYER CAKE

The secret to eternal youth is arrested development.

ALICE ROOSEVELT LONGWORTH

It is utterly false and cruelly arbitrary to put all the play and learning into childhood, all the work into middle age, and all the regrets into old age.

MARGARET MEAD

 There was a star danced, and under that was I born.

WILLIAM SHAKESPEARE

There is no cure for birth and death save to enjoy the interval.

GEORGE SANTAYANA

Sugar in the gourd and honey in the horn, I never was so happy since the hour I was born.

ANONYMOUS

Every human being on this earth is born with a tragedy, and it isn't original sin. He's born with the tragedy that he has to grow up . . . a lot of people don't have the courage to do it.

HELEN HAYES

'Tis education forms the common mind,
Just as the twig is bent, the tree's inclin'd.

ALEXANDER POPE

When the first baby laughed for the first time, the laugh broke into a thousand pieces and they all went skipping about, and that was the beginning of fairies.

JAMES M. BARRIE

Very early, I knew that the only object in life was to grow.

MARGARET FULLER

June

BIRTHSTONE — *Pearl: Health*
FLOWER — *Rose*
COLORS — *Light Blue and White*
GEMINI — *May 22 to June 21*
CANCER — *June 22 to July 22*

June comes with its roses red and white;
May its days be happy from morn till night.

Happy Birthday Clowns

3 PINTS ICE CREAM,
  ASSORTED FLAVORS
12 3-INCH ROUND
  COOKIES
36 COLORED JELLY BEANS
6 STRANDS RED LICORICE

1½ CUPS SHREDDED
  COCONUT
  GREEN FOOD
  COLORING
12 SUGAR ICE-CREAM
  CONES

🍃 The day before, on a flat plate, freeze 12 round scoops of ice cream for the clowns' heads. Buy or bake the cookies.

🍃 Assemble the clown faces by placing the cookies 2 inches apart on a serving tray. Top each with a scoop of ice cream. Use jelly beans to make the eyes and nose; cut licorice for the hair and mouth.

🍃 To tint the coconut light green, toss it in a bowl with a few drops of food coloring. Press the coconut around the bottom of each ice-cream face to make a fluffy collar.

🍃 Top each clown with an ice-cream cone hat. Store in the freezer until time to serve.

MAKES 12 SMILING CLOWNS

Born on Monday,
Fair in face;
Born on Tuesday,
Full of God's grace;
Born on Wednesday,
Sour and sad;
Born on Thursday,
Merry and glad;
Born on Friday,
Worthily given;
Born on Saturday,
Work hard for your living;
Born on Sunday,
You will never know want.

ANONYMOUS

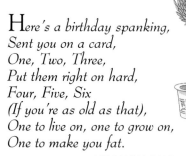

Here's a birthday spanking,
Sent you on a card,
One, Two, Three,
Put them right on hard,
Four, Five, Six
(If you're as old as that),
One to live on, one to grow on,
One to make you fat.

ANONYMOUS

Sing a song of Birthdays
Full of fun and cheer
And may you keep on having them
For many a happy year.

ANONYMOUS

ENGLISH	*Happy birthday!*
ARABIC	*Eed melad saïd!*
CHINESE	*Sāang yaht faai lokik!*
DANISH	*Hjertelig til lykke medfødselsdagen!*
DUTCH	*Hartelijk gefeliciteerd metje verjaardag!*
FRENCH	*Bonne fête!*
GERMAN	*Herzlichen glückwunsch zum geburtstag!*
HUNGARIAN	*Boldog szuletes napot!*
ITALIAN	*Buon compleanno!*
JAPANESE	*Otanjyobi omedeto!*
RUSSIAN	*Sdnyom rozhdenya!*
SPANISH	*Feliz cumpleaños!*
WELSH	*Penblwydd hapus!*

Thirty days hath September,
April, June, and November;
All the rest have thirty-one,
Excepting February alone,
And that has twenty-eight days clear
And twenty-nine in each leap year.

ANONYMOUS

31

July

BIRTHSTONE — *Ruby: Contented Mind*
FLOWER — *Larkspur*
COLORS — *Green and Russet*
CANCER — *June 22 to July 22*
LEO — *July 23 to August 23*

July makes us think of the red, white, and blue;
Forget-me-nots mean I'm thinking of you.

Pineapple Upside-down Cake

1½ CUPS SIFTED CAKE FLOUR
2 TEASPOONS BAKING POWDER
½ TEASPOON BAKING SODA
¼ TEASPOON SALT
12 TABLESPOONS BUTTER
½ CUP PACKED LIGHT BROWN SUGAR

1 CAN (20 OUNCES) PINEAPPLE SLICES IN UNSWEETENED JUICE
10 MARASCHINO CHERRIES
⅔ CUP GRANULATED SUGAR
2 LARGE EGGS
2 TEASPOONS VANILLA
½ CUP SOUR CREAM

❧ Preheat oven to 325° F. Set out a deep 10-inch ovenproof skillet. Sift the flour with the baking powder, baking soda, and salt. Reserve.
❧ Melt 6 tablespoons of butter in the skillet. Add the brown sugar, stirring until bubbly. Remove from heat.
❧ Drain the pineapple slices, reserving the juice, then arrange in the skillet with the cherries, cut in half, flat sides up.
❧ In an electric mixer, cream remaining butter with granulated sugar until light. Beat in eggs, one at a time, then 3 tablespoons of the juice, and the vanilla. Stir in the flour, alternating with the sour cream. Spoon over pineapple.
❧ Bake 30 minutes, until tester comes out clean. Cool 5 minutes before inverting onto a platter.

MAKES 8 SERVINGS

After all, tomorrow is another day.

MARGARET MITCHELL

All my possessions for one moment of time.

QUEEN ELIZABETH I

Nearly all the best things that came to me in life have been unexpected, unplanned by me.

CARL SANDBURG

You grow up the day you have your first real laugh at yourself.

ETHEL BARRYMORE

Make hay while the sun shines.

PROVERB

One to-day is worth two to-morrows.
BENJAMIN FRANKLIN

The more things change, the more they remain the same.

ALPHONSE KARR

Every ten years a man should give himself a good kick in the pants.

EDWARD STEICHEN

If only I may grow: firmer, simpler—quieter, warmer.

DAG HAMMARSKJÖLD

We are always the same age inside.
GERTRUDE STEIN

August

BIRTHSTONE — *Sardonyx: Conjugal Felicity*
FLOWER — *Gladiolus*
COLORS — *Orange and Red*
LEO — *July 23 to August 23*
VIRGO — *August 24 to September 23*

36

August brings days of recreation;
May you, too, have a glad vacation.

Ice-cream Sandwiches

3 SQUARES
  UNSWEETENED
  BAKING CHOCOLATE
2¼ CUPS SIFTED FLOUR
½ TEASPOON BAKING
  SODA
¼ TEASPOON SALT

1 CUP BUTTER
1 CUP SUGAR
1 LARGE EGG
1 TEASPOON VANILLA
2 TABLESPOONS MILK
1 QUART ICE CREAM,
  ANY FLAVOR

♣ To make the cookies, preheat oven to
350° F. Butter 2 baking sheets.
♠ Melt the chocolate over low heat and cool.
♥ Mix the flour with the baking soda and salt.
♣ Using an electric mixer, cream the butter
and sugar. Beat in chocolate, egg, and vanilla.
♥ Stir in the flour mixture, alternating with
the milk.
♠ Drop by tablespoonfuls, 3 inches apart, onto
baking sheets. Flatten each cookie with back
of spoon into a 2-inch circle. Bake 10 minutes
or until set. Let cool on pan for 3 minutes,
then remove to racks and cool for 30 minutes.
♣ Remove ice cream from freezer 15 minutes
before assembling sandwiches, to soften a bit.
Fill two cookies with the ice cream. Freeze for
½ hour before serving.

MAKES 15 ICE-CREAM SANDWICHES

The heyday of woman's life is the shady side of fifty.

ELIZABETH CADY STANTON

Thirty, thirty-five, forty, all had come to visit her like admonitory relatives, and all had slipped away without a trace, without a sound, and now, once again, she was waiting.

EVAN S. CONNELL

I am long on ideas, but short on time. I expect to live to be only about a hundred.

THOMAS ALVA EDISON

Forty is the old age of youth; fifty is the youth of old age.

FRENCH PROVERB

At twenty years of age, the will reigns; at thirty, the wit; and at forty, the judgement.

BENJAMIN FRANKLIN

A man of forty today has nothing to worry him but falling hair, inability to button the top button, failing vision, shortness of breath, a tendency of the collar to shut off all breathing, trembling of the kidneys to whatever tune the orchestra is playing, and a general sense of giddiness when the matter of rent is brought up. Forty is Life's Golden Age.

ROBERT BENCHLEY

 40

You make me chuckle when you say that you are no longer young, that you have turned twenty-four. A man is or may be young to after sixty, and not old before eighty.

OLIVER WENDELL HOLMES, JR.

No one over thirty-five is worth meeting who has not something to teach us,—something more than we could learn by ourselves, from a book.

CYRIL CONNOLLY

You take all the experience and judgment of men over fifty out of the world and there wouldn't be enough left to run it.

HENRY FORD

September

BIRTHSTONE — *Sapphire: Love*
FLOWER — *Aster*
COLORS — *Brown*
VIRGO — *August 24 to September 23*
LIBRA — *September 24 to October 23*

September brings asters and goldenrod gay;
May they brighten your path along life's way.

Tiny Tea Sandwiches

THINLY SLICED BREAD, WHITE OR BROWN	RIPE TOMATOES
SOFT UNSALTED BUTTER	SALT
CRACKED BLACK PEPPER	WATERCRESS SPRIGS
SOFT CREAM CHEESE	CUCUMBERS
	FRESH DILL
	HARD-BOILED EGGS
	MAYONNAISE
	FRESH CHIVES

❧ Trim the crusts from the bread.

❧ Blend the butter with pepper to taste. In another bowl, season cream cheese with pepper.

❧ For Tomato Sandwiches, blanch the tomatoes and peel. Place 1 thin tomato slice on bread spread with seasoned butter, and salt.

❧ For Watercress Sandwiches, put watercress on bread spread with seasoned butter.

❧ For Cucumber Sandwiches, thinly slice the cucumber and place on bread spread with seasoned cream cheese, snipped dill, and salt.

❧ For Sliced Egg Sandwiches, place egg slices on bread spread with mayonnaise. Sprinkle with chives or top with a watercress sprig.

❧ Cut each sandwich diagonally into four triangles. Set on a platter and cover with a damp cloth until time to serve.

MAKES A PERFECT BIRTHDAY LUNCH
SERVED WITH AN ASSORTMENT OF TEAS

How unspeakably the lengthening of memories in common endears our old friends!

GEORGE ELIOT

To me, fair friend, you never can be old,
For as you were when first your eye I ey'd,
Such seems your beauty still.

WILLIAM SHAKESPEARE

Time draweth wrinkles in a fair face, but addeth fresh colors to a fast friend.

JOHN LYLE

Friendship is the shadow of the evening, which strengthens with the setting sun of life.

JEAN DE LA FONTAINE

An old man loved is winter with flowers.

GERMAN PROVERB

A friendship counting nearly forty years is the finest kind of shade-tree I know.

JAMES RUSSELL LOWELL

Middle age is when you've met so many people that every new person you meet reminds you of someone else.

OGDEN NASH

I love everything that's old: old friends, old times, old manners, old books, old wines.

OLIVER GOLDSMITH

We are so fond of one another, because our ailments are the same.

JONATHAN SWIFT

October

BIRTHSTONE — *Opal: Hope*
FLOWER — *Calendula*
COLORS — *White and Yellow*
LIBRA — *September 24 to October 23*
SCORPIO — *October 24 to November 22*

October with gay leaves dancing along;
May it bring you a joyous harvest song.

Rainbow Cupcakes

3 CUPS SIFTED CAKE
  FLOUR
1 TABLESPOON BAKING
  POWDER
½ TEASPOON SALT
1 CUP BUTTER
2 CUPS SUGAR

5 LARGE EGGS
1 TABLESPOON VANILLA
1 CUP MILK
2 TEASPOONS GRATED
  ORANGE PEEL
  WHITE FROSTING
  FOOD COLORING

❧ Preheat oven to 350° F. Butter standard muffin tins or line with fluted paper cups.

❧ Sift the flour, baking powder, and salt.

❧ Using an electric mixer, cream the butter and sugar until light. Beat in the eggs, one at a time, then the vanilla.

❧ Stir in the flour mixture, alternating with milk. Stir in orange peel. Spoon batter into muffin tins, filling them three-quarters full.

❧ Bake 20 minutes or until tester comes out clean. Cool on a rack for 5 minutes. Remove from pans and cool completely.

❧ Frost with your favorite white frosting, tinted with a drop or two of various food colorings.

MAKES 24 CUPCAKES

Grow old along with me!
The best is yet to be, . . .

ROBERT BROWNING

For he's a jolly good fellow,
For he's a jolly good fellow,
For he's a jolly good fellow,
Which nobody can deny.

TRADITIONAL SONG

You will recognize, my boy, the first sign of old age: it is when you go out into the streets of London and realize for the first time how young the policemen look.

SIR SEYMOUR HICKS

What could be more beautiful than a dear old lady growing wise with age? Every age can be enchanting, provided you live within it.

BRIGITTE BARDOT

Try to keep your soul young and quivering right up to old age.

GEORGE SAND

To see a young couple loving each other is no wonder; but to see an old couple loving each other is the best sight of all.

WILLIAM MAKEPEACE THACKERAY

There are days of oldness, and then one gets young again.

KATHERINE BUTLER HATHAWAY

At middle age the soul should be opening up like a rose, not closing up like a cabbage.

JOHN ANDREW HOLMES

Middle age is when you still believe you'll feel better in the morning.

BOB HOPE

The perceptions of middle age have their own luminosity.

GAIL SHEEHY

November

BIRTHSTONE — *Topaz: Fidelity*
FLOWER — *Chrysanthemum*
COLORS — *Dark Blue and Red*
SCORPIO — *October 24 to November 22*
SAGITTARIUS — *November 23 to December 21*

November means Thanksgiving, too;
I'm thankful I have a friend like you.

Coconut Layer Cake

3¼ CUPS SIFTED CAKE
   FLOUR
 4 TEASPOONS BAKING
   POWDER
½ TEASPOON SALT
 1 CUP BUTTER

1¾ CUPS SUGAR
 6 LARGE EGGS
 1 TABLESPOON VANILLA
 2 CUPS LIGHT CREAM
 1 CUP FLAKED
   COCONUT

❧ Preheat oven to 350° F. Butter three 9-inch
round pans and line bottoms with waxed paper.
❧ Sift flour with baking powder and salt.
❧ Using an electric mixer, cream the butter
and sugar until light. Separate the eggs. Beat
in the yolks, one at a time, then the vanilla.
❧ Stir in the flour mixture, alternating with
the cream. Stir in the coconut.
❧ In another bowl, beat the egg whites until
stiff. Gently fold into the butter mixture.
Spoon evenly into pans.
❧ Bake 30 minutes or until tester comes out
clean. Cool on rack for 5 minutes. Remove
from pans and cool completely.
❧ Frost each layer and sides with Coconut
Lemon Frosting on page 53.

MAKES 12 SERVINGS

What I wouldn't give to be seventy again!

OLIVER WENDELL HOLMES, JR.

Live as long as you may, the first twenty years are the longest half of your life.

ROBERT SOUTHEY

In a dream you are never eighty.

ANNE SEXTON

Age is not measured by years. Nature does not equally distribute energy. Some people are born old and tired while others are going strong at seventy.

DOROTHY THOMPSON

The first hundred years are the hardest.

WILSON MIZNER

There must be a day or two in a man's life
when he is the precise age for something
important.

FRANKLIN P. ADAMS

Sixteen candles make a lovely light
But not as bright as your eyes tonight.

LUTHER DIXON

The lovely thing about being forty is that you
can appreciate twenty-five-year-old men.

COLLEEN MCCULLOUGH

At seventy-seven it is time to be earnest.

SAMUEL JOHNSON

At twenty-one, so many things appear solid,
permanent, untenable.

ORSON WELLES

A HAPPY
BIRTHDAY

December

BIRTHSTONE — *Turquoise: Prosperity*
FLOWER — *Narcissus*
COLORS — *Indigo and Green*
SAGITTARIUS — *November 23 to December 21*
CAPRICORN — *December 22 to January 21*

52

December and holly come always together;
May your Christmas have perfect weather.

Coconut Lemon Frosting

1 CUP BUTTER
2 TEASPOONS GRATED
LEMON PEEL
⅛ TEASPOON SALT
4 CUPS SIFTED
CONFECTIONERS'
SUGAR

⅔ CUP HEAVY CREAM
3 TABLESPOONS FRESH
LEMON JUICE
2 CUPS FLAKED
COCONUT
ALMONDS, SLICED

❧ Soften the butter to room temperature.
❧ Using an electric mixer, cream the butter, lemon peel, and salt in a large bowl until light.
❧ With the mixer on low speed, blend in the sugar and cream. Increase the speed to high and beat until light and fluffy. Beat in the lemon juice.
❧ Use to frost Coconut Layer Cake on page 49, sprinkling with the flaked coconut as you go. Place almonds on top.

MAKES ENOUGH FROSTING FOR
ONE 3-LAYER CAKE

Please don't retouch my wrinkles. It took me so long to earn them.

ANNA MAGNANI

One compensation of old age is that it excuses you from picnics.

WILLIAM FEATHER

Old age is not for sissies.

MALCOLM FORBES

To me, old age is always fifteen years older than I am.

BERNARD M. BARUCH

A man is old when he can pass an apple orchard and not remember the stomachache.

JAMES RUSSELL LOWELL

In the midst of winter, I finally learned that there was in me an invincible summer.

ALBERT CAMUS

If you survive long enough, you're revered— rather like an old building.

KATHARINE HEPBURN

Old age isn't so bad when you consider the alternative.

MAURICE CHEVALIER

They tell you that you'll lose your mind when you grow older. What they don't tell you is that you won't miss it very much.

MALCOLM COWLEY

A man is getting old when he walks around a puddle instead of through it.

R. C. FERGUSON

My candle burns at both ends;
It will not last the night;
But, ah, my foes, and, oh, my friends—
It gives a lovely light!

EDNA ST. VINCENT MILLAY

Once I was looking through the kitchen window at dusk and I saw an old woman looking in. Suddenly the light changed and I realized that the old woman was myself. You see, it all happens on the outside; inside one doesn't change.

MOLLY KEANE

Wrinkles should merely indicate where smiles have been.

MARK TWAIN